Thomas Barton

The conduct of the Paxton-men, impartially represented

Thomas Barton

The conduct of the Paxton-men, impartially represented

ISBN/EAN: 9783337147051

Printed in Europe, USA, Canada, Australia, Japan

Cover: Foto ©Andreas Hilbeck / pixelio.de

More available books at **www.hansebooks.com**

The PAXTON - MEN,

Impartially reprefented;

The DISTRESSES of the FRONTIERS, and the COMPLAINTS and SUFFERINGS of the PEOPLE fully ftated ; and the Methods recommended by the wifeft Nations, in fuch Cafes, ferioufly confider'd.

WITH SOME

REMARKS upon the NARRATIVE,

Of the Indian-Maffacre, lately publifh'd.

nterfpers'd with feveral interefting Anecdotes, relating to the MILITARY GENIUS, and WARLIKE PRINCIPLES of the People call'd QUAKERS : Together-with proper Reflection and Advice upon the whole.

n a LETTER from a GENTLEMAN in one of the Back-Counties, to a FRIEND in Philadelphia.

—— ——— Si tibi vera videtur,
Dede Manus ; et, fi falfa eft, accingere contra.———
LUCRET.

The impious Man who fells his COUNTRY's FREEDOM,
Makes all the Guilt of Tyranny his own.———
His are her SLAUGHTERS, her OPPRESSIONS His.———
MARTYN's TIMOLEON.

Whoever will pretend to govern a People without regarding them, will foon repent it;----Such Feats of Errantry may do perhaps in ASIA :---- But in Countries where the People are FREE, it is Madnefs to rule them againft their Wills.----They will know that Government is appointed for their Sakes, and will be faucy enough to expect fome Regards and fome Good from their own DELEGATES.----Thofe Nations who are govern'd in Spite of themfelves, and in a Manner that bids Defiance to their Opinions, their Interefts; and their Underftandings, ----are either SLAVES, or will foon ceafe to be SUBJECTS.
CATO's LETTERS.

PHILADELPHIA:

Printed by A Steuart, and fold by JOHN CREAIG, Shopkeeper in Lancafter. 1764.

from a GENTLEMAN in one
ier-Counties, to his Friend in Phi-
:lating to the Paxton-Men.

N RIOT (as it is called) makes fo great a
1 is fo much the general Topick, that a Man
: in Converfation, without having his Opi-
ning this Affair.——In Truth, Matters are
h a Pafs, that fome People are of Opinion,
ur to make them worfe may probably be
ςe them better. Refentment rages high,
: from every Quarter; and where it will
ε to thofe that have more *Light within them*,
of, to determine.
I am no Adept in Politicks, and have but
my Head about that Science, beyond the
imon News-Paper.—— It has long been my
be a Spectator of the Diftreffes and Suffer-
w Subjects; my Heart has often bled for
should ftill have continued a fecret Mourner
ot Power to redrefs, had not the unaccouta-
your City Quakers provoked me to fpeak
and unburthen myfelf to my Friend.—By my
1 as Situation in Life, you know, my dear
no political Ends to ferve; that I have no-
fear from Party Connections; and that I
ιer View in troubling you with this Let-
ε the miferable Frontier People, who lately
om the Infamy and Odium thrown upon
hofe unfeeling Hearts have never fuffered
rond their own private Intereft and Party. (*a*).
The

of this Letter, hopes he will not be underftood as
People's having taken up Arms. Such violent Steps
e productive of any thing, but WILD UPROAR and
itever therefore can have a Tendency to promote
the *leaft Infult* to the LAWS and GOVERNMENT of
ill ever think it his Duty to bear his Teftimony,
ountenance by every Means in his Power.

The INSURGENTS themſelves hand about a Kind of *Mani-feſto*, which contains the following Declaration, Grievances, Complaints, &c.———viz.

'That a trifling Diſpute, between a few Engliſh and
' French Traders upon the *Ohio*, was neglected; the profer'd
' Mediation and Aſſiſtance of the Indians to end the Quarrel,
' and the Proprietary-Offer of £.400, for erecting a ſmall
' Fortification there, together with £.100 yearly, towards
' the Support of it, were contemptuouſly rejected, *(b)* till it
' kindled the Flames of War, which at laſt ſpread and raged
' over half the Globe.— That from the Neglect of the *Legiſ-
' lative Part* of this Province, and the horrid Doctrines of
' *Non-Reſiſtance* at that Time ſo ſtrenouſly maintain'd, ſuch
' Calamities enſued, that near *one Hundred Miles* of as thriv-
' ing a Settlement as any in Pennſylvania has been reduced to
' Deſolation; many of the Inhabitants murdered or carried
' into Captivity, and the Reſt often drove from their Habi-
' tations in the utmoſt Diſtreſs and Want.— And beſides
' theſe particular Effects of this War, ſome of the beſt Blood
' in Chriſtendom has been ſpilt in it— whole Kingdoms
' have been almoſt depopulated; and Miſery and Ruin en-
' tail'd upon Millions of their Fellow Creatures.

' That even in the Midſt of this Deſolation and Carnage,
' every publick Meaſure was clogg'd— the King's Demands
' for Men and Money procraſtinated— unneceſſary, or at
' leaſt ill-timed Diſputes, about *Proprietary Inſtructions and
' Taxes*, were brought upon the Carpet, in Order to divert the
' Reproach and Diſhonour which the Province, thro' Quaker
' Meaſures, had incurr'd, and throw the whole Blame of the
' War at the *Proprietary* Doors. *(c)* And that this villainous
' Scheme might carry with it a better Face, the late infamous
' TEDYUSCUNG was treated with, and employed to charge
' the Proprietaries with having defrauded the Indians of ſome
' Lands, and to declare that this was the Occaſion of all
' their Uneaſineſs and Enmity to the *Engliſh*.—But infamous as
' TEDYUSCUNG was, he own'd at laſt that his Complaints were
' unjuſt; publickly renounc'd his Claim, and declared in open,
' Treaty

(b) See Governor MORRIS's Meſſage of November 22, 1755.
(c) See the Speeches and Meſſages between the Governer and Aſſem-bly, from the Year 1733, to the Year 1760.

' Treaty that he was urged to act this bafe Part, and that
" he was only the *Mouth of fome Perfons* in *Philadelphia;*
" whom he did not chufe to name." *(d)*

' That they have always manifefted, and are ftill upon
' every Occafion ready to manifeft their Allegiance and Loy-
' alty to their moft gracious Sovereign King GEORGE, whom
' they have ever efteemed as the kind and careful Father of
' his People.'

' That tho' born to Liberty, and all the glorious Rights
' and Privileges of BRITISH SUBJECTS, they were denied
' Protection, at a Time when the Cries of Murder and Diftrefs
' might have made the very Stones relent; and tho' roufed
' to Vengeance and eager to maintain and defend their Lives
' and facred Rights, their Hands were bafely tied up !'

' They could obtain no proper Law to collect their Strength;
' nor any Sanction or Encouragement to purfue the Ene-
' mies of their Country !'

' That they have fuffered and bled in the Caufe of their
' Country, and have done more to protect it from the Vio-
' lence of a rapacious Enemy than any others in the Pro-
' vince.'

' That agreeable to the Command of the Prophet, they
' have " fought for their Brethren, their Sons, and their
' Daughters, their Wives and their Houfes."—— That in
' this Conteft, many of them have loft their deareft Relatives;
' their Houfes, their Lands, their all; and from a plenti-
' full independent People have been reduced to Mifery and
' Want.'

' That they have been treated as *Aliens* of the Common-
' Wealth, and denied a juft and *proportionable Share in Legiflation:*
' For that out of 36 Members which the eight Counties in the
' Province fend to Aflembly, the three Counties of *Philadel-*
' *phia, Chefter* and *Bucks,* where the Quakers are chiefly
' fettled, return 26 of that Number; while the 5 remaining
' Counties, where thefe LORDLY RULERS could have no
' Chance of getting elected, are fuffered to fend but the
' other Ten.'

' That by this iniquitous Policy, the Inhabitants of thefe
' free Frontier-Counties, altho' a great Majority, have been
                                                      rendered

----
(d) This he declared at the laft Treaty at *Lancafter.*

' rendered unable to act in Defence of their Lives and Pro-
' perties; and therefore have lain for above eight Years at
' the Mercy of a cruel Savage Enemy and an unrelenting
' Quaker Faction : Whereas had they been jufty reprefented
' in Legiflation, inftead of prefenting PACIFICK ADDRESSES
' to the Affembly, telling them that " the raifing large Sums
" of Money, and putting them into Hands of COMMIT-
" TEES, who might apply them to Purpofes inconfiftent
" with their PEACEABLE TESTIMONY, was in its Confequen-
" ces deftructive of RELIGIOUS LIBERTY'.' (e) Inftead of
' doing this, I fay,— the firft great Law of Nature, that of
' SELF-DEFENCE, would have been adminiftred to the Peo-
' ple upon the firft Alarm of Danger, and the Hands of the
' HARDY and the BRAVE would have been fet at Liberty,
' til they had taken ample Vengeance of their MURDERERS.

' That they have often, in the moft fuppliant Manner,
' laid their Grievances before the Affembly ; and inftead of
' being redrefs'd, have been abufed, infulted, and even by
' fome Members of that *venerable Houfe*, deem'd as unwor-
' thy of Protection, as " A Pack of infignificant SCOTCH-
" IRISH, who, if they were all *killed*, could well enough be
" fpared." (f)

' That whilft they were thus abufed, and thus ftript of
' their *Birth-Rights*,——ISRAEL and JOSEPH, two pet-
' ty Fellows, who ought to have no higher Claims than
' themfelves, were permitted to lord it over the Land;
' and in Contempt of the Government, and the ex-
' prefs Orders of the Crown, forbiding them to hold
' private Treaties with the Indians, exchange Belts of Wam-
' pum with them—make them Prefents—all this they have
' done, and in their own Name, without fo much as in-
' cluding the fimple MENONISTS, from whom they had
' extorted large Sums of Money to Support this Expence.

' —— Nay, even with the moft matchlefs Impudence,
' infinuated to the Indians that they were Rulers and Go-
' vernors; as plainly appear'd at the late Treaty at LAN-
CASTER,

(e) See the Quaker-Addrefs to the Affembly, November 6, 1755.
(f) This unchriftian and ungenerous Speech was made by N———L
G.—B, a Quaker, Member of Affembly for *Chefter* County, and fome
others.

' CASTER, where the Principal CHEIF and SPEAKER told
' Mr. H——N, then Governor, "That as he underſtood
" there were two GOVERNORS in the Province, he would
" be glad to know which of them he was to treat with."*(g)*
' That the Indians were induced to look upon ISRAEL
' as the *firſt Man*, *or* CHEIF SACHEM of the Province,
' from ſeeing the Haughtineſs and Contempt with which
' he treated his Fellow Subjects, and his inſolent and ar-
' rogant Behaviour to Sir W——M J——N at *Eaſton*;
' and to Governor H——N, at *Lancaſter* : And that this,
' among other Things, has been productive of manifold
' Evils, by weakening our Credit with Indians, fruſtrating
' the good Intention of holding Treaties with them, and
' encouraging them, after they return'd from us loaded
' with Money, Cloaths, Arms and Ammunition, to look
' with Contempt upon us as a puſillanimous Pack of *old*
' *Women*, divided among ourſelves, without SPIRIT or
' RESOLUTION to call them to an Account, let them
' commit what Outrages they pleaſed upon us.———
' That they have been made Tributaries to ſupport the
' immenſe Expence of *Indian Treaties*; to which they
' chearfully ſubmitted, in Hopes that their dear Relati-
' ons and Fellow Subjects, who have been long detained
' in barbarous Captivity, would have been reſtored; But
' that inſtead of *inſiſting* upon the Promiſes and Engage-
' ments made by the Indians to this End, an extenſive
' and valuable Trade was opened with theſe faithleſs
' and

(g) That you may be convinc'd that ſuch was the Opinion of the *Indians*, I muſt obſerve to you, that one PATRICK AGNEW, of the Borough of *Lancaſter*, White-ſmith, having been duly ſworn upon the
HOLY EVANGELISTS, before the CHIEF BURGESS of that Town,
hath depoſed and ſaid, That he, the ſaid Deponent, being a Conſtable at
the laſt Indian Treaty at *Lancaſter*, was commanded by the *Governor*,
to proclaim, that no Perſon ſhould ſell or give any Kind of ſpirituous
Liquors to the Indians, on any Pretence whatever ; that he proclaim'd
this Order thro' the Town accordingly ; and that upon his making Proclamation, and ſaying, *by Order of the Governor*, an Indian named TE-
DYUSCUNG, cry'd out " D——n your G———r, D——n your G———r ;
" P-m—t-n is my Governor, P-m—t-n is our Governor, he allows RUM
" enough ;" and offer'd Violence to this Deponent ; who alſo, upon his
Oath, declares that, notwithſtanding the Proclamation, the Indians
were privately entertain'd at a certain Tavern in the Town.

' and perfidious Villains; and their poor unhappy Friends
' left to spend perhaps the Remainder of their days,
' in all the Sorrow and Miseries of *Heathinism* and *Bar-*
' *barity*, and to bow their Necks to the cruel Slavery of
' Savages.'

' That at a Time when their ungenerous and merciless
' Enemies, had again, without the least provocation, in-
' vaded the Province, with the very Arms and Ammuni-
' tion which they received at the late Treaties ; and
' when the Frontiers were yet reeking with the Blood
' of their slaughter'd Inhabitants ; and the murdered Ghosts
' of their Friends and Relatives cry'd aloud for Vengeance, a
' Number of Indians (many of which were concerned in this
' horrid Butchery) were escorted to the *Metropolis*, and there
' protected, cherished, and maintained in Luxury and Idle-
' ness, whilst they, the poor Sufferers, were abandoned to
' Misery, and left to starve, or beg their Bread.

' That upon seeing themselves thus abused and thus ne-
' glected, and considering that the Influence of a *Quaker Fac-*
' *tion* was the Source from whence all these Evils flow'd ; and
' that *pretended* Scruples against War and Fighting were the
' Root from whence all their Calamities and heavy Suffer-
' ings sprang, and if yet permitted, might produce worse
' and more heavy, they were determined to bear no longer.

' That *Pennsylvania* appear'd to them to be really in a
' dangerous CACHEXY ; and that at such a Crisis they
' look'd upon it as their Duty to administer such Remedies
' (however severe they might be look'd upon by some) as
' might raise her drooping Head, and restore her to Health
' and Vigour.——And should their first Trial fail of Suc-
' cess, that in that Case they are determined to *double the*
' *Potion*, (b) which they hope will intirely purge off the pec-
' cant Humours, restore the Solids, and secure her hereafter
' from the Infection of *Quaker Non-Resistance:*'

Such is the Declaration, and such the Complaints of these
People,——And indeed nine Tenths of the Inhabitants
of

(b) By this Expression, I am told, these People mean, that they
will renew their Application and ADDRESSES, with DOUBLE the
NUMBER of Signers ; and it is said, they are likely to get TEN to
ONE, that they had before, to *remonstrate* with them.

of the Back-Counties either tacitly, or openly, approve and support them——Every cool and well thinking Man, as well as Men among themselves, are sensibly concern'd that they were reduced to the Necessity of having Recourse to such Methods as might be deem'd an Insult to the Government and Laws of their King and Country.

The Names of RIOTERS, REBELS, MURDERERS, WHITE SAVAGES, &c. (i) have been liberally and indiscriminately bestowed upon them : But all this they look upon only as the Effects of disappointed Malice, and the Resentment of a destructive FACTION, who see their *darling Power* in Danger.——The *Merciful* and the *Good* however, they trust, will rather pity than condemn them.— And they are pleased with the Thoughts that they have been able at last to lay bare the PHARASAICAL BOSOM of QUAKERISM, by obliging the Non-RESISTING QUALITY to take up Arms, and to become Proselytes to *the first great Law of Nature.*

But this Triumph of theirs is founded upon a false Supposition, that *Quakers* never us'd Arms before.—— Whereas, it can be prov'd that these People have *taken up Arms,* and *fought well too,* upon many other Occasions.— Whoever will take the Trouble to read the printed Trials of G. KEITH, will find, that when a *Quaker*-Sloop, belonging to *this* Province, was formerly taken by some *PIRATES,* and finding it impossible to save both the *Sloop,* and their so much-cried-up *Principle, against outward Force,* they at last resolved to give up the *Principle,* rather than the *Sloop!* and so opposed Force to *Force*—retook their Vessel, and made some of the *Pirates* Prisoners !

It is plain that the first *Quakers* were never against Force of Arms, if *they* thought the Quarrel just.

If you will believe their own Writers, they fought well in the Reign of OLIVER CROMWELL.——G. *Fox,* in the Fifth Page of his Letter directed " *To the Council of Officers of the Army, &c.*" complains, That many *Quakers* were disbanded out of the Army, for no other Fault than their being *QUAKERS,* though *they* were good *Fighters* and good *Soldiers.*

B

" Many

(i) See the NARRATIVE, and a Letter from 'SQUIRE READ, the JERSEY DEMOSTHENES, &c.

" Many valiant Captains, Soldiers and Officers, fays he,
" have been put out of the Army by Sea and Land, of whom
" it hath been faid among you, that they had rather have
" had *One* of Them, than *Seven* Men, and could have
" turn'd out *one* of them to *feven* Men, who, becaufe of
" their Faithfulnefs to the Lord God, and it may be for
" faying *Thou* to a particular Perfon, and for wearing their
" *Hats*, have been turn'd out from among you."

This fame Mr. *Fox*, in a Book publifh'd by him and fome
others of his Brethren, intitled, WEST *anfwering to the*
NORTH, Page 96, 97, exults in thefe Words,— " Multi-
" tudes of People flock'd up to *Weftminfter* to complain of
" their Sufferings—which CHARLES STUART call'd *Tumults*;
" and by the Guard one of them was flain, at the Place of
" the fhedding of whofe Blood, CHARLES STUART's Head
" was ftruck off."———Thus their Enemies are punifhed.

In Page 102 are thefe Patriotick Expreffions, ——— " The
" righteous Ends of War 's for Liberty and Laws."———
And in Page 16 they boaft— " The Defence of them (the
" Laws) have we in the late Wars, vindicated in the Field,
" with our Blood."

One *Bifhop*, a Quaker Writer, in a Letter of his to the
Council of State, in the Time of the *Ufurpation*, written in the
Year 1650, advifes them in thefe Words, " It concerns you,
" while ye have Time, to bear down this *Enemy*, (meaning
" the King) and to fecure Places neceffary for *Defence*."—
And again he urges them to *kill* all that fhould appear in
Favour of the Royal Caufe ; " Do Juftice, fays he, on thofe
" whom God hath given into your Hands, left out of this
" SERPENT's EGG do come a COCKATRICE, and his Fruit
" be a fiery flying *Serpent*."———And in Page 26 he tells
them, " There is a Neceffity for the continual marching of
" your *Horfe* up and down in all Parts, efpecially where
" thefe INSURRECTIONS have been."

George Fox, in his COUNCIL and ADVICE, a Letter wrote
by him to O. *Cromwell*, dated the 11th Month, 1659, Page
26, 27, &c. tells him, That if he had been directed by his
Advice, " The HOLLANDERS (fays he to him) had been
" thy Subjects—GERMANY had given up to thy Will—
" The SPANIARD had quivered like a dry Leaf—The *King*

" *of*

" of *France* should have bowed under thee his Neck—The
" Pope should have withered as in the Winter—The Turk,
" in all his Fatnefs, should have fmok'd— Thou should'ft
" have *crumbled Nations* to Duft———Therefore, (fays he)
" let thy Soldiers go forth with a free and willing Heart,
" that thou mayeft *rock Nations as in a Cradle.*"

Robert Rich, another Author, informs us, That in the
Ufurpation, *Friends* had fuch an Intereft, that by the Act of
Parliament, bearing Date *June* 25th, 1650, for fettling the
Militia, the Quakers were made Commiffioners to form
Troops and *Regiments*; to nominate the *Officers*; and to af-
fefs Money for buying *Horfes, Arms, &c.*— He names Five
by their Names, whom he knew, who were of the Com-
mittee for the *Militia* of *Weftminfter*.

But *Friends* will deny all thefe Things. —— And if you
turn over to the Place, and fhew them the very Expreffions,
they will ftill endeavour to evade you, and will fneer at your
Ignorance for taking them in a *literal Senfe*, and tell you
with a very grave Phyz, that they are all to be taken *fpi-
ritually.*

If any Man has a Mind to be impofed upon by fuch
Quibbles, I have no Objection——Let him believe that no
more is meant here, than *fpiritual Soldiers—fpiritual Armie's
—fpiritual Wars—fpiritual Regiments and Militias!*——Let
him believe *fpiritual Troops*, and *fpiritual Horfe* too, if he
will !———*Si vult decipi, decipiatur.*

Mr. *Barclay*, the great Apoftle of Quakerifm, has indeed
taken great Pains in his *Apology*, to quote the Teftimonies of
the *Fathers* againft *Fighting* :—— And in Page 515 lays
down this Propofition, " That it is not lawful for Chriftians
" to refift Evil, or to make war *in any Cafe.*"

But did not your *Philadelphia Quakers* take up Arms, and
declare they would fight in *one Cafe*, namely, In Defence of
Friend Indians?

Therefore, thefe Quakers of Philadelphia have furely either committed a Thing *unlawful for Chriftians*; or belied
their Apoftle, and done Defpite to the Spirit of *Barclay*.—
Again in Page 558, *St. Robert* fays, " Whoever can recon-
" cile this, *refift not Evil*, with, *refift Violence by Force*;
" *Give alfo thy other Cheek*, with, *Strike again*; whoever
" (fays

" (fays he) can find a Means to reconcile thefe Things,
" may be fuppofed alfo to have found out a Way to recon-
" cile *God* with the *Devil*, *Chrift* with *Antichrift*, *Light*
with *Darknefs*, and *Good* with *Evil*.

But did not your Philadelphia Quakers, inftead of *Refift not Evil*, attempt to *Refift Violence by Force*: and inftead of *Give alfo thy other Cheek*, even plant Cannon
(and furely not Spiritual Cannon) in Order to Strike again?
They opened their moft noted Meeting-Houfe in Philadelphia to the Soldiers; and devoted it to War and Revenge.

What can we fay or think of fuch People as thefe?——
I am fure, if their peaceable and meek Apoftle could
come upon the Earth again, and fee his *Efteemed Friends*
become like other Men, and " clafhing with the Pot-
" fheards of the Earth. (*k*) "— he would blufh and difown
them as his Difciples.

In fhort, it is evident from the late Conduct of *Friends*,
that the *Peaceable Teftimony* which they have fo long
born to the World, at the Expence of the Lives and
Properties of Thoufands of their Fellow Subjects, is now
no more-----and that they have no more Scruple againft
taking up Arms, and Fighting than any others——Nay,
that they can go into more violent Meafures to *Refift Evil*
than perhaps were ever hear'd of in the moft *Warlike
Nations.*——

Where do we find or read of an Inftance of *Trenches* being
thrown up, and *Cannon* planted, to oppofe an infignificant
Mob?——And yet this was done by your *Philadelphia
Quakers*, againft a Handful of *Freemen* and the *King's Subjects*,
who thought it their Duty to kill a Pack of villainous, faithlefs Savages, whom they fufpected, and had Reafon to believe, were Murderers, Enemies to his *Majefty*, his Government, and Subjects——Were fuch violent Proceedings confiftent with the Principles which *Quakers* have profeffed to the
World? Were they confiftent with the Lenity and Mercy
of an *Englifh* Conftitution? Surely No.—— Such fevere Meafures will never do with a free People, who conceive themfelves

---

(*k*) A Phrafe made ufe of by a QUAKER TEACHER, to his Con-
gregation in *Philadelphia*, in exhorting them to adhere to their PEACE-
BLE PRINCIPLES.

felves oppreffed.——— Even *France* and *Spain*, notwithftanding the arbitrary Government and fevere Laws eftablifhed in
them, are not without their *Infurrections* and *Tumults*———
I hope it will not be fufpected that I am a Favourer or En-
courager of Mobs and Riots——I folemnly declare I have as
great an Averfion to Mobs, and all riotous Proceedings, as'
any Man can have, as any Man ought to have (*l*)— But at
the fame Time, I muft own, I fhall never be for facrificing
the Lives and Liberties of a free People to the Caprice and
Obftinacy of a deftructive Faction.

Whoever will examine the Proceedings and Debates of
Parliament, efpecially thofe in the Year 1737, will find the
Sentiments of the wifeft and braveft People under Heaven,
concerning Tumults and Riots.—As thefe Things were in-
troduced into the Debates of that Seffion, I fhall trouble you
with a few Extracts of the Speeches on that Occafion.

Lord C——T declared himfelf thus— ' The People (fays
' he) feldom or never affemble in any riotous or tumultuous
' Manner, unlefs when they are oppreffed, or at leaft ima-
' gine they are oppreffed. If the People fhould be miftaken, and
' imagine they are oppreffed, when they are not, it is the Duty
' of the *Magiftrate* to endeavour firft to correct their Miftake
' by fair Means and juft Reafoning; in common Humanity
' he is obliged to take this Method, before he has Recourfe
' to fuch Methods as may bring *Death* and *Deftruction* upon
' a great Number of his Fellow-Countrymen ; and this Me-
' thod will generally prevail, where they have not met with
' any real Oppreffion : But when this happens to be the Cafe,
' it cannot be expected that they will give Ear to their Op-
' preffor; nor can the fevereft Laws, nor the moft rigorous
' Execution of thofe Laws, always prevent the People's be-
' coming tumultuous :———You may fhoot them—— You
' may hang them— But till the Oppreffion is removed or al-
' leviated, they will never be quiet, till the greateft Part of
' them are deftroyed. The only effectual Method to fupprefs
' Tumults will be, to enquire into the Caufes, and to take
' fuch Meafures as may be proper for removing thofe Caufes :
' For in the *Body Political*, as in the *Body Natural*, while the
' Caufe remains, it is impoffible to remove the Diftemper.'

Lord

(*l*) See the firft Note upon this Letter.

'Lord B——st fpoke to this Effect—' The chief End
', of a Parliamentary Enquiry is not to *difcover* or to *punifh*
'. the Perfons concerned in any Tumult ; it is the Conduct
' of the *Magiftrate* that we are principally to enquire into ;
' and if upon fuch Enquiry, it fhould appear, that the Tu-
'. mult was occafioned by any unjuft or *Oppreffive Conduct*, or
', by *Negligence* and *Indolence*, we ought to cenfure or to punifh
· fuch a Magiftrate——Such an Enquiry, and fuch an Iffue on
'. Enquiry, will fatisfy the People, it will remove the Caufe
' of Tumults, and confequently will prevent them for the
' future : Whereas if we employ ourfelves folely in difco-
', vering and punifhing the Rioters, we do not remove but
', encreafe the Caufe of Tumults ;— we fhall make the Peo-
' ple more difcontented than they are—The Severity of the
' Punifhment may fear up the Wound for a Time, but it will
' not be healed{; it will fefter, and endanger the total Diffo-
' lution of the Political Body.'

' By thefe Kind of Proceedings (fays another noble Lord)
' we may for a While keep the People quiet, or knock out
' the Brains of thofe who fhall prefume to be otherwife ; but
' we fhall never remove their Difcontents, or gain their Af-
' fections ; and this muft be done, or our Government muft
' be made Arbitrary ; for a free Government cannot be fup-
' ported but by having the Affections of the Generality of
' the People.'

Now, Sir, had your Quakers, thofe *Children of Peace*,
adopted thefe wife Sentiments, and purfued thefe humane
juft and truly politic Meafures, every Thing might have
been eafy. But inftead of this, they neglected and defpifed
the Complaints of an injured and oppreffed People; refufed to
redrefs their Grievances ; they promoted a *military Apparatus* ;
fortify'd the Barracks ; *planted Cannon*, and ftrutted about in
all the Parade of War, as if they chofe rather to have the
Province involv'd in a Civil War, and fee the Blood of perhaps 5 or 600 of his Majefty's Subjects fhed, than give up,
or banifh to their native Caves and Woods, a Parcel of
treacherous, faithlefs, rafcally Indians, fome of which can
be proved to be Murderers. But if they were all innocent, by
what Law are we obliged to maintain 140 idle Vagabonds ?
Muft *Pennfylvania* work for murdering Savages as their
Lords and Mafters ?   But

But in the Name of Wonder! What could be meant by ill thefe warlike Preparations ? Surely the Quakers did not intend to make Ufe of *Mufquetry* and *Cannon* too, in cafe the *Rioters* had proceeded ! If they did, they muft either be very ignorant or very defperate and cruel——It has often been declared in Parliament, That ‘ the Liberty of Firing at Random, upon any Multitude of his Majefty’s Subjects, is a Liberty which ought to be moft cautioufly granted ; and never made ufe of but in Cafes of the moft abfolute ‘ Neceffity——And in this Way of thinking (fays one of ‘ the great Speakers upon the Subject) I am fupported by ‘. the whole Tenor of the Laws of England—— It is now 2 ‘ or 300 Years fince *Fire-Arms* came in Ufe amongft Us, ‘ yet the Law has never fuffered them to be made Ufe of by ‘ the common Officers of Juftice——Pikes, Halberts, Battle- ‘ Axes, and fuch like, are the only Weapons that can be ‘ made Ufe of according to Law by fuch Officers.—— It is ‘ well known that by a late Statute, which is in Force in ‘ *Scotland* as well as in *England* ; the Power of the Civil ‘ Magiftrate, in the Cafes of any Mob or riotous Affembly, ‘ is fully and diftinctly regulated ; yet even by that Law ‘ (which I have often heard complained of as a Law not to- ‘. lerable in a free Country) there is no exprefs Order given ‘ to the Magiftrate or his Affiftants, to make Ufe of *Fire-* ‘ *Arms* ; fo cautious was the Legiflature of giving a legal ‘ Authority for making ufe of fuch Weapons.

‘ I know it will be faid that Officers of Juftice and their Af- ‘ fiftants, efpecially his Majefty’s Troops, when they hap- ‘ pen to be called to the Affiftance of the Civil Magiftrate, ‘ are in a very unlucky Situation, if they are not allowed to ‘ make ufe of the Arms in their Hands to prevent their be- ‘ ing knocked on the Head——Their Situation, I fhall ‘ readily grant, may be unlucky enough ; but we are to ‘ confider the Law as it ftands ; and as the Law ftands in ‘ *England* as well as in *Scotland*, if a Perfon fuffers Death by ‘ *firing*, the Perfon that fired, and he who gave him Orders ‘ to fire, might both be profecuted for *Murder* ; and I am ‘ afraid neither of them would have any Refourfe, but in the ‘ King’s Mercy.—— The Soldiers may upon fuch Occafions ‘ make Ufe of their fcrew’d Bayonets, for difperfing or feiz-

‘ ing

' ing the Rioters ; by fo doing they can hurt none but thofe
' that refift them ; but I would not advife them to *fire*, un-
' lefs they fhould find themfelves in very great Danger of be-
' ing overpower'd, and perhaps murdered by the Mob."

Such was the Senfe of the greateft Men in England, and fuch the Caution and Lenity of a Britifh Parliament.

But what will the World fay, or Pofterity think of your meek and peaceable Quakers, who thro' pretended Scruples againft Refiftance! thro' Obftinacy and Love of worldly Power, which they themfelves would neither apply to the Ends for which it ought to be ufed, nor refign into the Hands of thofe that would; who have fo long fuffer'd the Province to bleed beneath the *Savage Knife*, its faireft and moft fruitful Fields to be deluged in Gore, and laid wafte and defolate by *Barbarian Spoilers!* when they have been frequently fupplicated, entreated and conjured, by all the ties of brotherly Love, Friendfhip, Humanity and Juftice, to confider the Mifery and Diftraction of their Country------but could never be prevailed upon to ftand up in its Defence, or to ufe proper Means to refcue it from thefe fad Calamities: Yet have lately appeared with Arms and all the *dread Machinery of War*, to fight their beggar'd, ruined, miferable Fellow Subjects; and to afford that Protection to their cruel Enemies and Murderers, which their Unhappy Countrymen, in their moft deplorable Circumftances, could never obtain from them?——O ungenerous, unfeeliug Men! Was this the way to treat a ruined, defparing People?-----Will not Religion, Reafon, Humanity, Juftice, Charity, anfwer No?——Who was it that reduc'd them to the difagreable Neceffity of proceeding in the Manner they did?——From what Source are they to derive their Mifery? and, Who was it that provok'd and moved them to Refentment? Who is it that has made them Rioters, and then Reproaches, and defires they may be *Shot* or *Hang'd* for being fo? Who is it that has thrown fo many Obftacles in the Way of their Protection and Security? Who is it that has fcreened and fupported the Enemies of their Country, and pours out Vengeance and Deftruction upon thofe that attempt to chaf-

tife

tife and punifh them ? Thefe are Queftions which every
Body, with a Moments Refle&ion, may anfwer.

A mighty Noife and Hubbub has been made about killing a few Indians in Lancafter-County; and even *Philofo-
phers* and *Legiflators* have been employed to raife the Holloo
upon thofe that killed them ; and to ranfack *Tomes* and *Sy-
ftems*, Writers ancient and modern, for Proofs of their Guilt
and Condemnation ! And what have they proved at laft ?
Why, that the WHITE SAVAGES of *Paxton* and *Donnegall*
have violated the Laws of Hofpitality ! I can fincerely af-
fure the ingehious and worthy Author of the NARRATIVE,
that a Shock of *Electricity* would have had a much more fen-
fible Effe& upon thefe People than all the Arguments and
Quotations he has produced.

For my own Part, I utterly abhor and difclaim every
A& and Species of Cruelty, and I do folemnly declare,
that I difapprove of the Manner of killing the Indians
in *Lancafter*, as it was a Kind of Infult to the Civil
Magiftrates, and an Encroachment upon the Peace and
Quiet of that Town ; and I wifh that the *Women* and *little
Ones* at leaft, could have been fpared.——But no doubt
the A&ors in that Affair, thought with *Friend Bifhop*, whom
I quoted before, that the beft Way was, while their Hands
were in, to *kill all*, " left out of the SERPENT's EGG,
" there fhould come a COCKATRICE, and his Fruit fhould
" be a fiery flying SERPENT."

However, Matters of this Kind will always be told with
fhocking Aggravations---- I am perfuaded had not Things
been mifreprefented, fome Circumftances in the *Narrative*
would never have been fent into the WORLD.

The Public have indeed received *there* a very *amiable*
Chara&er of thefe Indians, and have been told that " The
" Univerfal Concern of the neighbouring white People on
" hearing of their being killed, cannot well be expref-
" fed." Now I have been frequently inform'd, for many Years, by fundry of their neareft Neighbours in the
Caneftogoe Mannor, that they were a *drunken, debauch'd,
infolent, quarrelfome* Crew : and that ever fince the Com-
mencement of the War, they have been a Trouble and
Terror to all around them—as for *Will Soc* and his Bro-

C   ther,

ther, I am told there are undoubted Proofs of their Guilt
and Treachery— That they have threatened and drawn their
Knives upon People who have refused to comply with
their Demands, is a Fact well known to Hundreds. *(m)*
The

(m) ABRAHAM NEWCOMER, of the County of *Lancaster*, one of the
People call'd *Menonists*, and by Trade a Gun-smith, hath personally appeared before the Chief-Burgess of Lancaster, and upon his solemn Affir-
mation hath declared, "That divers Times within these few Years,
" BILL Soc and INDIAN JOHN, two of the *Caneftogoe Indians*, threaten-
" ed to *scalp* him, for refusing to mend their Tomahawks, and swore
" they would *scalp* him, the *Affirmant*, as soon as they would a *Dog*."
He further affirms, " that a few Days before the Indians were kil-
" led in the *Mannor*, *Bill Soc*, aforesaid, brought a Tomahawk to him
" to be steel'd, which this *Affirmant* refusing to do, the said *Bill Soc*
" threatened, and said, *you will not! you will not!— I'll have it mended
" to your Sorrow.*— From which Expressions this *Affirmant* hath de-
" clared, that he apprehended Danger from said *Soc*."
Mrs. T—P—N, a Lady of Character, of the Borough of *Lancaster*,
also personally appear'd before the Chief-Burgess, and upon her solemn
Oath on the Holy Evangelists, hath declared, " That sometime in the
" Summer of the Year 1761, *Bill Soc* came to her Appartment, and
" threaten'd her Life, saying, *I kill you, and all Lancaster cannot catch
" me;* which put her into great Terror. And this Lady hath further
" depos'd, that said *Bill Soc*, added, *this Place* (meaning *Lancaster*) *is
" mine and I will have it yet.*"
Capt. JOHN HAMBRIGHT, a Gentlemen of Reputation, and an emi-
nent Brewer of the Borough of *Lancaster*, personally appeared before
ROBERT THOMPSON, Esq; one of the Justices for the County of *Lancaster*, and made Oath on the Holy Evangelists, that " about August,
" in the Year One Thousand, Seven Hundred and Fifty-Seven, he,
" this Deponent, being an Officer in the Pay and Service of the Pro-
" vince of *Pennsylvania*, was sent with a Party from Fort *Augusta* to
" Hunter's, for Provision for that Garrison : That on his Way down he
" halted, under cover of the Bank of the River *Susquehanna*, to rest and
" refresh his Men, at M'*Kee*'s old Place, having a Centry fixed on the
" Bank, behind a Tree, to prevent a Surprize : That the Centry, after
" some time, informed that there were Indians coming up the Road ;
" upon which this Deponent crawled up the Bank, and discovered two
" Indians, one of which he knew to be *Bill Soc* (one of the Indians lately
" killed at *Lancaster*:) That he suffered them to come pretty near, and
" then discovering himself, called to *Bill Soc* to come to him, imagin-
" ing he was going, as usual, to Fort *Augusta*, where he had often
" seen him among the Indians: That the Indians then immedi-
" ately halted, and after consulting about a Minute, ran off with
" their greatest Speed, which at that Time much surprized this Depo-
" nent, as the said *Soc* had always pretended Friendship, and no Violence
" or

The Public are also informed, that " The Magistrates " of Lancaster sent to collect the remaining Indians,— brought " them into the Town, comforted and promised them Pro- " tection. "——— If they did this, they must be very silly indeed—For how was it possible for Men destitute of a MILITIA, without Men, Arms, or Ammunition to protect them ?— But I am credibly informed that the Truth of the Matter was, That

---

' or Threats were then offered to them, and neither this Deponent or ' his Party had any Intentions to injure them : That upon this Depo- ' nent's proceeding down to Hunter's, he was informed that an old Man ' had been killed in that Neghbourhood the Day before ; and, as no ' other Mischief was at that Time done in those Parts, nor no Account ' of any other Indians being seen or heard of, on that Quarter, at that ' Time, the said Bill Soc, and his Companion, a strange Indian, were suf- " pected and believed to be the perpetrators of that Murder. That he ' this Deponent, before this Time, had frequently seen Bill Soc with ' his Brothers and others of the Coneſtogoe Indians, at Fort Augusta, and ' often met them on the Communication, carrying up Kegs of Whisky ' and other Things, to trade with the other Indians there ; but that af- ' ter this Murder the said Bill Soc did not appear at that Garrison for ' near four Months, and then came there with a Number of other In- ' dians from up the River above the Fort ; at which Time he behaved ' in a different Manner than usual, not coming into the Fort, nor being ' so familiar as formerly." And further this Deponent saith not.

Sworn and subscribed, the 28th of)   JOHN HAMBRIGHT
    February 1764, before me   )
        ROBERT THOMPSON.

CHARLES CUNNINGHAM, of the County of Lancaster aforesaid, per- sonally appeared before THOMAS FOSTER, Esq; one of the Magistrates or said County, and being duly qualified, according to Law, doth depose. and say, That " he (the said Deponent) heard an Indian, named Joshua ' James, say, since the last War, that he never killed a white Man in ' his Life ; but six Dutchmen that he killed in the Minisinks." And arther saith not. Sworn and subscribed before THOMAS FOSTER, by
        CHARLES CUNNINGHAM.
N. B. Said Joshua James was one of the Coneſtogoe Indians.

ALEXANDER STEPHEN, of the County of Lancaster, personally appear- ed before THOMAS FOSTER, Esq; one of the Magistrates for said County, and being duly qualified, according to Law, doth depose and say, That " an ' Indian Woman, named Cannayah Sally, told the said Deponent, since the ' last War, that the Coneſtogoe Indians killed Jegrea, an Indian Man, ' because he would not go to war, with the said Coneſtogoe Indians, ' against the English : And that James Cottes told the said Deponent,
        " since

That thefe Magiftrates being apprehenfive of the Danger of the Indians, were very defirous to have them removed im-mediately to *Philadelphia*, as a Place of much greater Secu-rity—through which Negleſt to remove thither they muſt have loſt

---

" fince the laſt War, that he was one of the three that killed old *James* " (or *William*) *Hamilton*, on *Sherman*'s Creek, the Beginning of laſt War, " and another Man, with fix or feven of his Family. And farther " this Deponent faith, that after the late War, ſaid *James Cottes* de-" manded of ſaid Deponent a Canoe, which he had found, or Payment " in lieu thereof, which Canoe the ſaid Murderers had left, as *Cottes* " ſaid, at the Time ſaid Murder was committed." And farther ſaith not;

Sworn and ſubſcribed before THOMAS FOSTER, *by*

ALEXANDER STEPHEN.

N. B. *Jegrea* was an old Indian that had formerly been a Warrior, but had now quit going to War, and was threatning the *Conneſtogoe* In-dians, if they would go to War againſt the white People, and diffuad-ing and commanding them from it.

ANN-MARY LeROY, of the Town of *Lancaſter*, appear'd likewiſe before the Chief-Burgeſs, and being ſworn on the Holy Evangeliſts of Almighty GOD, did depoſe and ſay, " That in the Year 1755, when her " Father, JOHN JACOB LEROY, and many others were murdered by " the Indians, at the *Great Mahqnnoy*, ſhe, this Deponent, her Brother, " and ſome others were made Priſoners, and taken to the *Kittaning*Town, " and that during her four Years Captivity, the French Officers were fur-" niſh'd weekly, or once in two Weeks, with the *Pennſylvania* Gazette. " That ſhe ſaw ſtrange *Indian* Meffengers come frequently, whom the " French Officers and Interpreters told this Deponent, were the Caneſto-" goe *Indians*—and that at the ſame Time they affur'd this Deponent, that " the ENGLISH had not one *Indian* in their Intereſt, except ISAAC ; " and that the Caneſtogoe *Indians* were willing to take up the *Hatchet* a-" gainſt the ENGLISH, whenever the *French* would requeſt them to do " it "——This Woman hath moreover declar'd on her Oath, that ſince " her Return from Captivity, BILL SOC's reputed Mother came to her, " this Deponent, at Lancaſter, and after ſome Enquiry about the Indian " Family, with which ſhe was a Priſoner ; this Deponent aſk'd ſaid " SOC's Mother, if ſhe had ever been out in the Back-Parts ? who " replied, ſhe had not ; but that her Son BILL had been out often, and " would again : and that *he was good for Nothing* ; or Words to that " Effeſt." [THERE are many more Depoſitions (I am told) to the fame Purpoſe, which I have not ſeen. But ſurely theſe are ſufficient to " *ſatisfy the Publick*," that not only " *Will Soc, but the whole Tribe, were* " *really Guilty of thoſe Offences againſt us, which were laid to his Charge.*" And that " the Makers and Venders of theſe Accuſations can produce that " *Evidence*" which the Author of the NARRATIVE has ſo *publickly* call'd for.

The foregoing are true Copies of the Affidavits paſſed,

loft their Lives, and not through any Mifconduct of the Magiftrates—For it feems the Affair was accomplifh'd fo unex-
pectedly and fuddenly, that not one Half of the Magiftrates
knew any Thing of the Matter till they were all kill'd ; and
thofe that did, could do nothing, unlefs it was to go at
the Peril of their Lives, among an enraged and armed Multitude, and attack them with *Stones* and *Brickbats*.

I have indeed heard it alledged againft thofe Magiftrates,
that there were fome *Soldiers* in the Place, which they might
have called to their Affiftance— But I have heard it pofitively
declared, by many of the Inhabitants of that Town, who were
Eye-witneffes of the whole Tranfaction, that if there were
Ten Thoufand Soldiers difpers'd and ftrolling about in the Manner that thefe were at the Time, it would have been impoffible to have got them to their Arms, and properly drawn
up, before the Indians were killed ; fo dextrous and expe-
ditious were the PAXTONIANS in executing their Purpofe.

The Author of the *Narrative* proceeds with all the *Pathos*
of Language and Expreffion, and tells us, " That when the
" poor Wretches faw that they had no Protection nigh, they
" divided into their little Families, the Children clinging to
" their Parents ; --- They fell on their Knees, protefted
" their Innocence, declared their Love to the *Englifh*, and
" that in their whole Lives, they never had done them any
" Injury ; and in this Pofture they all received the Hatchet !
" Men, Women and little Children !"--- This was cruel indeed, if it was fo— But I would be glad to know who could
give this Gentleman fo very particular an Account——— I
have been told, that not a fingle Circumftance happened
which could have given rife to it ; and that the above Story
was pick'd up from among a Parcel of old Papers in a *Hop-
Garden* or a *Hemp-field* (I forget which) upon *Sufquehanna*.—
And indeed this feems moft likely to have been the Cafe : ---
For who could poffibly tell what pafs'd, or how thefe Indians
behaved in the fhort Interval between their being attacked
and all killed, which is faid not to have been above Two
Minutes : (n) No one had any Kind of Intercourfe with them,
nor even faw them during that Time, except thofe that killed

(n) It is confidently faid, that the PAXTONIANS were not above
twelve Minutes altogether in the Town, and not above two Minutes in
difpatching the Indians.

led them, and they declare, that not one of them appeared in that Posture, nor spoke a Word; and that if they had, it would have been impossible to have heard them for the Noise of the shouting of the Multitude.

It is also asserted in the *Narrative*, " That the Bodies of " the murdered were brought out and exposed in the " Street."—This appears likewise to have been misrepresentation—I have been informed by some of the most reputable Inhabitants of *Lancaster*, that they were never removed out of the *Work-house* and *Work-house-yard*, where they were shot, till they were brought out to be carried to their Graves.

The next Charge usher'd in by the *Narrative* to blacken these unhappy People, is, " That with the *Scriptures* in " their Hands and Mouths, they can set at nought that ex- " press Command, *Thou shalt do no Murder* ; and justify " their Wickedness by the Command given to *Joshua*, to " destroy the Heathen."—And then follows a dreadful Exclamation in these Words,—" Horrid Perversion of Scripture " and of Religion !" I am really amazed that the *Philosophic* Writer of this Paper should suffer himself to be so much impos'd upon, and influenc'd by the malevolent Tittle Tattle of every lying Sycophant. Every Body knows that this Aspersion is the reputed Offspring of the *Curled-Lock Lawyer*, who wrote the *Dialogue* between *Andrew*, *&c.*—A Creature, who by his Debaucheries, and immoral Life, has done more Dishonour to the Scriptures and Religion, than all these Men put together ; and who has been endeavouring for a Series of Years to sow the Seeds of Discord and Dissention among his Fellow-subjects, and has even in print propagated groundless and wicked Insinuations among the Germans, that the English intended to reduce them to a State of Vassalage and Slavery.(o)——Surely the *ex parte* Relations of this poor drunken Fellow should have been below the Notice of the worthy Author of the *Narrative*. But it seem-this Gentleman was determined to avail himself of any Thing that he thought might bring Infamy and Odium upon the *Paxton People* ; and for this End he has not scrupled to call the killing the Indians Murder !—— I should be glad to

(o) See some Papers published by him in the German Language, and dispersed thro' *Berks* County.

to know, who appointed him a Judge or Jury upon this Affair ? Does he find that the Government has call'd it *Murder* in either of the Proclamations he has quoted ? I have
already declared, that I difapprove of the Manner of killing
thefe Indians ; and yet I am perfuaded this Writer, with all
his Ingenuity, will find it too hard a Talk to prove it *Murder.*
The Faith of Government, we are told, was pledged to
thefe Indians---- No doubt of it :---- And fo it is to every
Robber and *Villain* before he becomes fuch : (*p*) But will any
Man fuppofe that a *Robber and Villain* fhould rely upon that
Faith, when he has forfeited it ; and claim Protection from
the *Gallows* or the *Gibbet,* or from being fhot down if he cannot be brought to Punifhment any other Way ? Now whatever might have been the Behaviour of thefe Indians to the
firft Settlers of *Pennfylvania,* it is notorious that their Conduct of late has been fuch, as could give them no Manner of
Claim to the Faith, Friendfhip, or Protection of this Government— That they have been Spies upon all our Actions
— have treacheroufly held a Correfpondence with our *avow-
ed* Enemies— and have often lent a helping Hand to bring
Ruin and Defolation upon the Province—and yet to fuch
Wretches as thefe, it feems we ow'd Protection !---- and it
was *Murder* to put them to Death ! The Author of CATO's
Letters very juftly obferves, that ' It is a moft wicked and
' abfurd Pofition, to fay, that a People can ever be in fuch
' a Situation, as not to have a Right to oppofe a *Tyrant,* a
' *Robber,* or a *Traitor,* who, by *Violence, Treachery, Rapine,*
' infinite *Murders* and *Devaftations,* has deprived them of
' Safety and Protection.'
' It was a known Maxim of Liberty amongft the great,
' the wife, the free Antients, that a *Tyrant,* or a *Traytor,*
' was a *Beaft of Prey,* which might be killed by a Spear as
' well as by a fair Chace; in his *Court* as well as in his *Camp*;
' that *every* Man had a Right to deftroy One, who would
deftroy

(*p*) Notwithftanding the folemn Engagements and Articles of Agree-
ment into which thefe Indians had entered with WILLIAM PENN, they
often broke thro' them, even in his Time.—In Governor KEITH's Time,
about the Year 1719, thefe Indians were accufed by one JOHN CART-
LIDGE, of many Mifdemeanors, and among the reft of having *furnifhed
our Enemies with Ammunition,* which obliged Mr. KEITH to write to
them, and threaten them, if they did not behave better. Thefe are
Facts well known to many now living.

' deftory all Men; that no Law ought to protect him who
' took away all Law; and, that like *Hercules*'s Monfters, it
' was glorious to rid the World of him, *whenever*, and by
' *what Means foever*, it could be done.'

' If we read the Stories of the moft celebrated Heroes of
' Antiquity, (Men of whom the prefent World is not wor-
' thy) and confider the Actions that gained them their high-
' eft Reverence and Renown, and recommended their Names
' to Pofterity with the moft Advantage, we fhall find thofe
' in the firft Rank of Glory, who have refifted, deftroy'd or
' expell'd *Traitors* and *Tyrants*, the *Pefts*, the *Burthens*, and
' the *Butchers* of Mankind.—— And indeed fuch an Action
' could never have been cenfured in the World, if there had
' not lived in all Ages, abject Flatterers, and fervile Crea-
' tures of Power, always prepared to fanctify and abet the
' moft enormous Wickednefs, if it were gainful: And thefe
' are they who have often mifled good Men in the worft
' Prejudices.'

' TIMOLEON, one of the wifeft and moft virtuous Men
' that ever bleffed the Earth, fpent a long and glorious Life
' in deftroying Tyrants: He killed, or caufed to be kill'd,
' his own Brother, in order to fave his Country.'

Did not the Roman Senators kill *Julius Cæfar*, even in the
Senate-Houfe, in order to free their Country of a Tyrant and
an Oppreffor? Did not *Brutus*, the Elder, put his own Sons
to Death for a Confpiracy to reftore *Tarquin?* Did not *Mu-
tius Scævola* gain immortal Honour for an Attempt to kill
Porfenna by *Surprize*, who was a foreign Enemy, making unjuft War upon *Rome?* Did not *L. Quintus Cincinnatus*, a
brave and virtuous Dictator of *Rome*, order *Spurius Mælius* to
be flain, though there was no Law fubfifting, by which he
could be put to Death; and though imploring the publick
Faith, to which he had been a Traytor and fworn Enemy.

Have we not read of Men who have killed themfelves, rather than become a Prey to a mercilefs Enemy —— *Brutus*
and *Caffius*, the *Decii*, *Otho*, *Celanus*, *Cato*, and many others,
have done this, prefering Death to Slavery.——Moft ftrange
then! that the killing of a few treacherous Savages, who by
their Perfidy, had forfeited their Lives, fhould be efteemed
fo enormous a Crime!—— But we are told that this Action
was

was a Breach of the Rites of *Hospitality*, which, *Heathens*, *Turks*, *Saracens*, *Moors*, *Negroes* and *Indians*, have held more facred than the PAXTONIANS. The Author here prostitutes his own good Senfe, and contrary to the known Rules of Logic and found Reafon, draws an univerfal Conclufion for particular Premifes: As well might he argue that *Goliah* was a Giant, and fo were all the Soldiers in the Army of the *Philiftines*; or *David* fpared *Saul* afleep in the Cave, and therefore he fpared all his Enemies.

Would the Limits I have prefcribed to myfelf in this Letter allow me, I could eafily fhew you, that every one of thofe Nations have, in a Thoufand Inftances, violated the Laws of Hofpitality, and Faith too, in a much higher Degree than thefe People could poffibly have been guilty of.— But without carrying you through *Homer*, old *Legends*, and *fabulous Travels* and *Voyages*—— if you look into your *Bible*, you will find a very notable Inftance, which will fet this Matter right.——We read in the 4th Chapter of *Judges*, that when *Ifrael* was fold into the Hands of *Jabin*, King of *Canaan*, the Captain of whofe Army was *Sifera*, who had nine hundred Chariots of Iron, and had mightily oppreffed the Children of Ifrael for 20 Years; the Lord at laft, by his Inftruments *Deborah* and *Barak*, delivered *Ifrael* from *Jabin* and *Sifera.*—" And the Lord difcomfited *Sifera*, and all his " Chariots, and all his Hoft with the Edge of the Sword, " before *Barak*; fo that *Sifera* lighted down off his Chariot, " and fled away on his Feet, to the Tent of *Jael*, the Wife " of *Heber* the *Kenite*: For there was Peace between *Jabin* " the King of *Hazor*, and the Houfe of *Heber* the *Kenite*.

" And *Jael* went out to meet *Sifera*, and faid unto him, " Turn in, my Lord, turn into me, *fear not*: And when " he had turned in unto her into the Tent, fhe covered him " with a Mantle," (or Blanket, as you find it exprefs'd in the Margin.)

" And he faid unto her, give me, I pray thee, a little " Water to drink, for I am thirfty; and fhe opened a Bottle of Milk, and gave him Drink, and covered him.

" Again he faid unto her, ftand in the Door of the Tent, " and it fhall be when any Man doth come and enquire of " thee and fay, Is there any Man here? that thou fhall fay, " No. " Then

D

" Then *Jael*, *Heber*'s Wife, took a Nail of the Tent,
" and took an Hammer in her Hand, and went foftly unto
" him, and fmote the Nail in his Temples, and faftened it
" into the Ground ; (for he was faft afleep and weary) fo he
" died."

Now was this Action (which has every Appearance of
Cruelty in it) deemed a Breach of Faith, or a Violation of the
Rites of Hofpitality ? No.—— In the 5th Chapter we find
the Angel of the Lord pronouncing a Blefling upon her ; no
doubt for ridding the World of an Oppreffor, and a cruel
Villain—" Bleffed above Women fhall *Jael* the Wife of *He-*
" *ber* the *Kenite* be, bleffed fhall fhe be above Women in
" the Tent.

" He afked *Water*, and fhe gave him *Milk*, fhe brought
" forth *Butter* in lordly Difh.

" She put her Hand to the Nail, and her right Hand to
" the Workman's Hammer ; and with the Hammer fhe
" fmote *Sifera*, fhe fmote off his Head, when fhe had
" pierced and ftricken through his Temples.

" At her Feet he bowed, he fell, he lay down, there he
" lay down dead."

In the *Apocrypha*, we have another Inftance no lefs re-
markable than the above——We find that *Judith* killed *Ho-*
lofernes even deceitfully, when it could be done no other
Way.——*Holofernes* was the chief Captain of the Army of
Affur, who made War againft *Ifrael* ; and when he was going out againft them, he threaten'd in thefe Words ;——" I
" will go forth in my Wrath, and will cover the whole
" Earth with the Feet of my Army, and I will give them
" for a Spoil unto them :—So that their Slain fhall fill their
" Valleys and Brooks, and the River fhall be filled with
" their Dead, till it overflow—And I will lead them Cap-
" tives to the utmoft Parts of the Earth."

But *Judith*, a Widow, of whom it was faid—" There was
" none that gave her an ill Word ; for fhe feared G O D
" greatly"—— I fay, this good Woman, having humbled
herfelf, and prayed to God to profper her Purpofe, went
over to the Camp of the Enemy ; and being taken by the
Watch and conducted to *Holofernes*, fhe declared to him that
fhe had fled from her own Nation—— " Now therefore, my
" Lord.

" Lord, (says she) I will remain with thee, and thy Servant
" will go out by Night into the Valley, and I will pray unto
" God, and he will tell me when they have committed their
" Sins.

" And I will come and shew it unto thee: Then thou
" shalt go forth with all thine Army, and there shall be
" none of them that shall resist thee.

" And I will lead thee through the Midst of *Judea*, un-
" til thou come before *Jerusalem*, and I will set thy Throne
" in the Midst thereof, and thou shalt drive them as Sheep
" that have no Shepherd, and a Dog shall not so much as
" open his Mouth at thee."

Yet notwithstanding these Declarations, we find that when
she was left alone in the Tent, and found *Holofernes* drunk,
and lying upon his Bed——" She came to the Pillar of the
" Bed which was at *Holofernes*' Head, and took down his
" Faulchion from thence, and approached to his Bed, and
" took hold of the Hair of his Head, and said, Strengthen
" me, O Lord God of Israel, this Day. And she smote
" twice upon his Neck with all her Might, and she took
" away his Head from him."

Upon which *Ozias* said unto her, " O Daughter, blessed
" art thou of the most high God, above all the Women
" upon the Earth; and blessed be the Lord God, which
" hath created the Heavens and the Earth, which hath di-
" rected thee to the cutting off the Head of the Chief of our
" Enemies.

" And God turn these Things to thee for a perpetual
" Praise, to visit thee in good Things, because thou hast
" not spared thy Life for the Affliction of our Nation, but
" hast revenged our Ruin, walking a straight Way before
" our God. And all the People said, So be it, So be it."

But no doubt it will be objected here, that these were not
Christians— And perhaps I might be challeng'd to produce
an Example from any " *civiliz'd Nation in Europe*"—— Lest
you should be prevailed upon to believe that it was not in my
Power to answer such a Challenge, I shall give you an In-
stance of the horrid Cruelty and Inhumanity of a *civilized
Nation*, whose Honour and Hospitality the Author of the
Narrative has taken great Pains to applaud and extol; and
I am

I am induced to point out this Fact in particular, as it happened in our own Time, and in our own Country.

In the Year 1746, or 1747, a *Spanish Privateer* entered the River *Delaware*, and proceeded almost up to *Newcastle:* The Crew went on Shore, and plundered two or more Plantations—On their Return they met with, and attacked, an *English* Ship commanded by Captain *Brown*, who gallantly defended himself, till being overpowered, he was obliged at last to strike and submit; but the *Spanish Officers* were so exasperated at the gallant and brave Defence he made, for which a generous and merciful Enemy would have esteem'd and honour'd him, that they barbarously *stabb'd* and *murder'd* him, tho' an humble Suppliant on his Knees, begging Quarter, and praying them to spare his Life!

What need I adduce any further Instances than these? If killing the Indians in *Lancaster* County, was a Violation of the Laws of *Faith* and *Hospitality*, I must then declare it, as my Opinion, that every Nation under Heaven, have been guilty of this Crime in a much higher Degree than the *Paxton People*, and with less Provocation.

The Author of the *Narrative* tells us, that " ONE HUN- " DRED and FORTY Indians yet remain (he should have said " are yet maintained, caressed and cherish'd) in this Go- " vernment."

I do not pretend to know the Motives of the Government for so doing; they perhaps knew little of the true Character of these Savages; perhaps they were hurried into it by the Importunities of a Faction; but this we firmly believe, that no other Colony on this Continent would chuse to follow their Example. The Province of *New York*, with great good Sense and Policy, and with a proper Spirit of of Indignation against such perfidious Wretches, refus'd them even a Passage through their Territories.—— But the *humane*, the *merciful*, the *charitable Pennsylvania*, can receive these *Villains* and *Murderers* into her Bosom, (q) disoblige three
Fourths

(q) It is well known to some of the Officers now in Philadelphia, that many of those Indians were engag'd against Colonel *Bouquet* and his brave Men.——The Murderer of *Stinton*, has been visited and comforted; a warm Bed and Stove have been set up for him, while many of our *Fellow-Christians*, less criminal than him, have been neglected; and left to
struggle

Fourths of her own Children, rather than part with them—make them Tributaries to support their Enemies in Luxury and Extravagance, whilft they themfelves have fcarce Bread to eat—and threaten to knock them on the Head, if they fhould offer to ftrike thefe *Darlings*, or even murmur at their hard Fate.——— Surely this is no aggravated Reprefentation, but a melancholly Fact !

Is it any Wonder then if the unhappy Frontier People were really *mad with Rage*, (as they exprefs themfelves) under fuch cruel Treatment ?——— Shall *Heathens*, fhall *Traytors*, fhall *Rebels* and *Murderers* be protected, cloathed and fed ? Shall they be invited from Houfe to Houfe, and riot at Feafts and Entertainments ? (r) Shall they be fupported in Eafe and Indolence, and provided with Phyficians and Medicines whenever they complain ?— And fhall the *free born Subjects of Britain*, the brave and induftrious Sons of *Pennfylvania*, be left naked and defencelefs—abandon'd to Mifery and Want —to beg their Bread from the cold Hand of Charity— and for

---

ftruggle with their Mifery and Chains, in the Dungeon.———That the *Moravian* Indians have been Traytors to us, is prov'd by the Depofition of one *Thomas Moore*, who being fworn on the Holy Evangelifts, before the chief Burgefs of *Lancafter*, has declar'd, that during his four Years Captivity with the Indians, they had frequent Intelligence and Advice of the Motions of the Englifh, from the *Bethlehem Indians*, who came conftantly among them, and kept up a Correfpondence with them.

   (r) It is faid that ISRAEL, that great Patron and Friend of Indians, hath kept his Houfe and Stable open for thefe Wretches and their Horfes, whilft the begger'd Frontier-People have been drove from his Door, without Pity or Relief.

It is well known that the Indians in this War, have cruelly maffacred our Traders, and feized their Goods ; and is it any Wonder, when they are reprefented by the Heads of a Faction (who inflamed the Indians at thefe Treaties againft the Traders) as Rogues that cheated them out of their Skins.

The following Anecdote was extracted from the DIARY of *Conrad Weifer*, Efq; written in his own Hand.

July 3d, 1760.

" Thefe Indians told me that the French Indian (fo they called him) " that was laft Winter in Philadelphia, pretending to be a Meffenger " from the *Ohio* Indians, reported on his Return, That the Quakers in " Philadelphia gave him a *Rod* for the Indians on *Ohio*, to *chaftife the Peo-* " *ple* fettling on the Indian's Lands on the other Side the Apalachin " Mountains ; and *to take Courage, the Majority of the People of Penn-* " fylvania *was on the Indians Side of the Queftion, and do difapprove of the* " *Proceedings of Onas in fettling the Indian Country.*"

for want of Medicine or Relief from a Surgeon or Phyfician, to linger out a miferable Life, and perifh at laft under the Wounds received perhaps from thefe very Villains ?———— My Soul rifes with Indignation at the Thought !— This is a Confideration that muft give Bitternefs to every humane Spirit, though it fhould fuffer no other Way than by Sympathy ! What good Man is there, whofe Heart does not bleed, when he fees a Set of Men amongft us embracing BARBARIANS, with more Tendernefs and Hofpitality than ever they fhew'd to their diftreffed Countrymen and Fellow-fubjects ?— When he hears them exprefs more Sorrow and Compaffion for the Death of a few *Savage Traytors*, than they ever expreffed for the Calamities of their Country, and the Murders of their Fellow-Chriftians ?— When he fees them take up Arms to protect thefe cruel *Monfters*, which they would never do to protect their own Neighbours and the King's Subjects, from the moft inhuman Butcheries ?————When a Waggon-Load of the fcalped and mangled Bodies of their Countrymen were brought to *Philadelphia* and laid at the *State-Houfe Door*, and another Waggon-Load brought into the Town of *Lancafter*, did they roufe to Arms to avenge the Caufe of their murder'd Friends ?—Did we hear any of thofe Lamentations that are now fo plentifully poured forth for the *Coneftogoe Indians ?*—— O my dear Friends ! muft I anfwer —No ? The *Dutch* and *Irifh* are murder'd without Pity.

I am no Stranger to your Fellow-feeling and Humanity :— I well know that you have a Tear for Diftrefs, and a Sigh for Mifery—— And if it were not criminal, I fhould envy you your happy Lot, in being placed by Providence at fome Diftance from the Scenes of Deftruction and Defolation, of which, I and my Neighbours have been melancholy Eye-Witneffes——To ufe the Words of the Poet ;

> ————*If we could recount*
> *Our baleful News, and at each Word's Deliverance*
> *Stab Poinards in our Flefh, till all were told,*
> *The Words would add more Anguifh than the Wounds.*
> SHAKESPEAR.

The Miferies of the back Inhabitants are really beyond the Power of Defcription— Nor are the dreadful Barbarities committed upon fuch of our unhappy Brethren as fell into
the

the Paws of the Enemy, to be equalled in all the Volumes of Hiſtory. Figure to yourſelf ſome Thouſands of Families, ſeated in Eaſe and Plenty, enjoying every Neceſſary of Life, which hard Labour and Induſtry had procured for them; without a Moment's Warning, and in the Shades of Night, driven from their Habitations; and obliged to flee through a lonely tractleſs Wilderneſs, without ſo much as knowing whither they directed their trembling Steps!—— When the Morning arrives— O what a Scene does it diſcover !— The Husband lamenting his murder'd faithful Wife !—The Wife tearing her Hair in all the Horror of Diſtreſs, ſhrieking, and calling upon her breathleſs Husband to haſten to her Relief! —*Rachael* weeping for her dear Children, who are now no more !— *Here* lies the provident Father welt'ring in his own Blood, his Scalp tore off, his Body ript up, his Bowels dragg'd out, and his private Parts ſtuffed into his Mouth !(s) —*There* the virtuous tender Mother lies ſtretched on her Bed, dreadfully mangled, with her new-born Infant ſcalp'd and placed under her Head for a Pillow, and a Stake drove into her - - - - - Modeſty forbids me to name it !(t)—— On *this Side* lie the Bodies of a numerous Family, half devoured by Wolves and Swine !(u)—On *that Side* lie the mangled Limbs of Men, Women, Children, and Brute Beaſts, promiſcuouſly ſcattered upon the Earth, (x)ſcarce to be diſtinguiſhed from one another !——Or perhaps the Bodies of theſe unhappy People, with their Horſes, their Cattle, their Houſes and their Grain, all burnt to Aſhes in one general Flame ! (z)

Who, my dear Sir, that ſees theſe Things, but muſt be filled with Grief and Horror ?——Or, *Quis*

(s) Theſe are no aggravated Scenes, in order to raiſe the Commiſſeration of the Reader; they are ſhocking Matters of Fact: It was done in the GREAT COVE.

(t) This was near *Shippensburg.*

(u) In Sheerman's Valley; all in Cumberland County.

(x) *James Smith*, Son of *Robert Smith*, late of Cheſter County, who was a Captive four Years and an half among the Indians, reports, that he at ſundry Times ſaw the Remains of mangled Bodies in the Woods, that were burnt by the Indians; and that the Captives told him they were Witneſſes to theſe horrid Cruelties exerciſed towards their Fellow Captives, ſometimes only for attempting to eſcape; and that this was done even by the Tawawaas, the gentleſt of the Savages.

(z) This was the diſmal Fate of Gnadenhutten, a *Moravian* Village, in Northampton.

Quis talia fando temperet à Lachrymis ?

I may well cry out in the Language of the NARRATIVE, " Unhappy People !—to have liv'd in fuch Times, and by " fuch Neighbours !"—— If the Characters of the feveral Nations, with which the Author of this Piece has fur- nifh'd us, be juft— I am fure thefe unhappy Frontier-People would have been fafer and better protected in any of thofe Nations, than they have been in a *Quaker Government*—— " They would have been fafer among the antient *Heathens*," by whom, it feems, " they would have been confidered as " *Guefts* of the Publick, and the Religion of the Country " would have operated in their Favour——They would have " been fafer, if they had fubmitted to TURKS," or had come under their Protection—" They would have been fafer a- " mong SARACENS, if they had once drank Water with " them—They would have been fafer among the MOORS of " SPAIN, if Faith had once been pledg'd to them, and a " Promife of Protection given— They would have been fafer " among POPISH SPANIARDS, if they had been in Dif- " trefs— They would have been fafer among the NEGROES " of AFRICA, where at leaft one manly Soul would have " been found, with Senfe, Spirit, and Humanity enough to " ftand in their Defence——In fhort, it appears that they " would have been fafe in any Part of the known World— " except in the Neighbourhood of the RELENTLESS and OB- " STINATE QUAKERS of PENNSYLVANIA !"

But Complainings (you will fay) cannot mend the Matter. ——What then is to be done !——Have there been any Re- medies provided againft future Misfortunes ?—— Muft thefe unhappy People ftill crouch beneath their Sufferings ?—— Or will not the Government go into any Meafures to redrefs them ?——It would be cruel as well as abfurd, to fuppofe it will not.——To ftifle the Notions of Revenge, is prudent and religious in private Perfons——And I hope thefe People will never again be reduced to the difagreeable Neceffity of proceeding as they did.———The *executive Part* of the Go- vernment, at leaft, deferves their Efteem and Affection. I truft therefore, they will never do any Thing that may bring their Obedience and Regards to the LAWS and MA- GISTRACY of their Country in Queftion.—— But at the
                                                                      fame

same Time, it is undoubtedly true, that a proper Spirit of Jealousy, and Revenge too, in a People who are oppress'd and injur'd, is a politick and commendable Virtue; without which they will never be valued or respected.———— Upon such Occasions, I think they should rouse the Spirit of a free People, and make it appear by all *lawful* and *loyal* Methods, that they scorn to be any longer the Property of a Faction——— And that they have a Right to *demand*, and to *receive* Protection.

Salus Populi suprema Lex esto ; is a Sentence that deserves to be written in Letters of Gold— It is a Sentence that should be the Motto of every Government, where Liberty and Freedom have any Existence.

We are told that in the *wise*, the *free* Cities of Athens and Rome, " *The awful Authority of the* People, *the sacred* " *Privileges of the* People, *the inviolable Majesty of the* People, *the unappealable Judgment of the* People, were common Phrases.

But it seems that there are Men in Pennsylvania, who (to use the Words of the great Algernon Sidney) look upon the People " like *Asses* and *Mastiff Dogs*, who ought " to *work* and to *fight*, to be *oppress'd* and *kill'd* for them."— And that they have neither *Privilege* or *Authority* to complain of their Sufferings, or remonstrate their Grievances.

However, I would have such Men know, that (whatever contracted Sentiments they may entertain) as a Patriot Writer justly observes, " It is the undoubted Right of the People, and acknowledg'd to be so in the *Bill of Rights* pass'd in the Reign of King Charles I. and since by the *Act of Settlement* of the Crown at the Revolution, to represent their publick Grievances, and to petition for Redress to those whose Duty it is to right them, or to see them righted : And it is certain, that in all Countries, the People's Misfortunes are greater or less, in Proportion as this Right is encourag'd or check'd."

It is indeed the best and only just Way that they can take to breathe their Grievances ; and whenever this Way has been taken even Kings have always accepted their Application.—— The Parliaments of Great-Britain too, who are the grand Barriers of our Liberty, have always

E   shewn

shewn themselves ready and willing to receive the Complaints of their Principals, and to apply quick Remedies to the Grievances contain'd in them.—— It has, indeed, been always thought highly imprudent, not to fay dangerous, to refift the Groans of the People, utter'd in this Manner.

This has been a Method, which has always had great Weight with good Men, and has always been a great Terror to Bad.———It has therefore always been encourag'd or difcourag'd, according to the Innocence or Guilt of Men in Power.

TITUS and TRAJAN, confcious of their own virtuous Adminiftration and worthy Purpofes, encourag'd Addreffes and Informations of this Kind, from their People:——They wifely knew, that if the ROMAN People had free Leave to *fpeak*, they would not take Leave to *act*;—— and that whilft they could have *Redrefs*, " they would not feek *Revenge*."

I fhall now conclude, Sir, with this Requeft to you, that you will advife your vifionary QUAKERS and DON QUIXOTES, to confider thefe Things——— And, that inftead of yoking themfelves to CANNON, and dragging them along to defend BARRACKS, and fight WIND-MILLS, they will fuffer the Complaints of the People to be heard, their Grievances redrefs'd, and their Country refcued from total Ruin.——That, they will immediately remove the INDIANS, or whatever elfe may create their Jealoufy, and give them Caufe to murmur. —— And then we may expect to feel the happy Effects refulting from LIBERTY and LAW—to fee the Quiet of the Province reftor'd—and the Harmony and good Order of Government re-eftablifh'd amongft us.

I am, &c.

Dated from my FARM-HOUSE, March 17th, 1764.
A Day dedicated to LIBERTY and ST. PATRICK.

F I N I S.